"THE DISTINCTIONS OF CHRIST"

BRAINSTORMING
TIMELY AND
IMPRESSIONABLE
IDEAS

GARRY R. THOMPSON

WESTBOW
PRESS®
A DIVISION OF THOMAS NELSON
& ZONDERVAN

WestBow Press books may be ordered through booksellers or by contacting:

WestBow Press
A Division of Thomas Nelson & Zondervan
1663 Liberty Drive
Bloomington, IN 47403
www.westbowpress.com
844-714-3454

Scripture taken from the King James Version of the Bible.

ISBN: 979-8-3850-3649-3 (sc)
ISBN: 979-8-3850-3650-9 (hc)
ISBN: 979-8-3850-3648-6 (e)

Library of Congress Control Number: 2024921957

Print information available on the last page.

WestBow Press rev. date: 10/30/2024

CONTENTS

INTRODUCTION

I arrived at many determinations upon which I have expressed and related throughout this book. They are truthful opinions gained from extensive research into related subject materials and studying many spiritual experiences throughout my life. Many of my observations were gained from relating life to what is stated in the Christian Bible, as well as comparing other religions texts to reality of human affairs since early civilizations on our earth. Rational reasoning and common sense and an elevated desire to know the full and absolute truth of our human condition in our Creator's presence drives me to share what I have learned with everyone.

Although human knowledge has increased exponentially and a multitude of mysteries have been revealed to the observant, there remains extremely many virtues to be exercised by the masses of mankind before true enlightenment will prevail over ignorance and errors of faulty desires.

Thus far in my life I have come to the 'idea' that in our God's whole creation, where mankind is the definite object of His desires and plans, it can be suggested that in essence of finality it is the judgments of right or wrong, or acts of good or bad in one's life, that results in the ultimate outcome or resulting condition of reward or punishment. One earns and experiences many pleasures and pains throughout their life on earth, and we must learn to manage these to our good throughout.

I have also come to the idea or conclusion that the righteous always suffer unjustly at the hands of the wicked, thereby the righteous gain grace and virtues and rewards for their patience and endurance, both on this earth, and are stored up for them in paradise upon their conclusion of the trials and tribulations they experienced since birth.

Whereas when the wicked persecute and oppress the righteous, our Creator allows them to go on and even prosper in their bad works. Because by so doing they are building up their iniquity to a full, whereupon man's Creator can justly consign them to appropriate punishments.

Upon further thought, my conclusion is that the righteous suffer for reward, whereas their wicked oppressors earn their damnation. So it must be that in our Creator's infinite knowledge and wisdom, He created it thus.

In this book I offer my sincere beliefs and honest opinions on religions and philosophies, as well as my ideas on the deceits of false salvation.

All the scriptures quoted in the text of this book are sourced from the official Authorized King James Version of the Christian Holy Bible.

AUTHOR'S BIOGRAPHY

Having a profound determination to succeed, and having experienced a lifetime of unfortunate mistakes and setbacks in an unstable and unforgiving world, it is my unswerving faith in my God that I have gained the experience necessary to the point where I recently wrote and published this book.

If there is anything I want to accomplish in my life, more than anything else in our wonderful world, it is to share with the readers of this book my collective knowledge of the ways of our world and of our God. What I have gained through trials and tribulations of this world, directed research, and cognitive development, is intimately revealed in this book, as I personally and diligently perceived them over many years.

It is my sincere desire to relate to individuals that we must stop and prevent the further deterioration of the many degenerating environmental factors at present on our planet, that can only end with a "World War 3" reality.

Unless remedial action is comprehensively taken very soon, our God's 'world of mankind' will be facing a whirlwind of tragedy, the likes of which mankind has never faced before, nor will mankind ever face it again.

I have enjoyed writing this book, and it my wish that each of you also in turn enjoy reading it.

It is my firm conviction that World War 3, or Nuclear Armageddon, can be avoided if enough of mankind change and amend our ways in God's favour, and for the benefit of mankind's disposition in our existence in our God's creation.

PREFACE

We citizens of our planet earth must quickly stop in the direction we are headed, especially now in these perilous and violent times, before the end is too close and World War 3 be upon us. We must reach out in determined faith and with a mentally astute mind and softened heart, and thoroughly embrace the truth of Christ in word and deed.

There exists no alternative to doing this with full purpose of heart, as we are at the precipice of a nuclear holocaust. With a vast majority of mankind threatened with a violent death by actual fire at any time these days, we must pool our resources and act decisively as one determined generation to accept God's sovereignty over mankind's affairs.

Only then will we begin to avoid the 'Nuclear Armageddon' that hangs over our heads that threatens total destruction of our planet, and only then will we begin to enjoy peace and the multitude of Christ's blessings He has stored up for us.

CHAPTER 1

UNIVERSAL MYSTERIES

Beyond Nothing To Infinite Paradise

1. What is beyond infinity?

Empty, dark, never ending, before time began, deepest of cosmic realities, infinite space, matterless and physicalness void, utterly without length, width, height or volume, no sound, no light, exclusivity to exist by inherent naturalist identity, just a supernatural 'intellectual' of paranormal dimensions, superior and utterly unnatural 'state of Being'.

2. What or who is this 'intellectual' or 'being'?

This 'intellectual' or utterly unnatural state of 'being' is and has always had awareness of it's (or 'His') own existence. This 'intellectual' knew at 'His' beginning (all knowing) He can only exist and continue to exist if 'He' is infinitely perfect throughout. As 'His' inherited eternity makeup and cosmic curvature (one epic event from beginning to end) demands perfect justice and infinitely perfect timing of all innumerable events throughout the entire cosmic event called the 'creation'.

3. **Was it possible for this 'intellectual' or 'being' to fulfill all of creation's infinite expectations and cosmic calculations?**

Yes! It was and is infinitely possible. As we speak, as He had not physical or material birth, but just existed solitary in infinite space, naturally and supernaturally just existing at His own will and pleasure ordained discourse. Master of all knowledge, judgment, wisdom, understanding, power and dominion, which He acquired by supernatural inherent disposition. By infinitely stating in the first act of seven creation days, He commanded: "Let there be light!" He commanded it, and caused it to come to pass throughout His celestial domain (the infinite universe). As the biblical account states, this was the first day of the Genesis creation account.

4. **Will we creatures of physical and material existence, and very limited lifespan, ever be able to comprehend the term 'infinity' and the fullness of it's meaning, as it applies to our visual universe surrounding us?**

Only the mentally, superior 'intellectual' or 'Being' can understand the infinite complexities of the length, width, height and volume that encompasses the space surrounding our earth. Time and space are fixed, stationary and exemplary according to the original guidelines our Creator manifested from before the beginning of the creation. The only purpose of the physical and material universe and earth was and is to provide a rearing circle for man and creature in which to dwell, each doing good and evil, and being judged accordingly. Mankind, some more than others as apportioned by this 'Being' and 'Judge', will hardly ever be elevated mentally or spiritually to fully comprehend the infinity of the 'intellectual' or

Being, Creator or Judge. Or to put it more simply, the infinity of our "God". We can understand the meaning of, and the concept of, no limits infinity. But it is beyond our mind's eye to visualize it mentally. I don't think it will ever be able to be done by man or creature. The creation, and every single event that takes place in it in the infinite universe from the beginning to after the ending is regulated, configured, maintained and all acts within it that are brought into existence and being, was, is and will be initiated by our God or "Creator"!

5. **What is this 'intellectual', or 'God', or 'Creator's' name if He is indeed a living "Being"?**

Many societies of mankind have come up with several different names for a god or creator they assumed to be their maker. Unfortunately, almost all of these were false gods, that had no basis or usefulness in reality. But one nation was chosen by our Creator, and they were the original Hebrew nationality. They called their Creator by His personal name in English 'Jehovah'. About 2,000 years ago, Jehovah took on Himself a body of human form of flesh and blood, and dwelt among His Hebrew nation. At that point He took on Himself a different, more precise and just name of "Jesus Christ".

6. **Why and how did this 'Being' or God come to live as a 'man-god' on earth and to what purpose?**

In the intricacies of the cosmic epoch or infinite creation, for our Creator's imperative to maintain His perfection, or otherwise fail the whole one and only effort, he created for Himself a guideline. And one that is universally applicable. "The demands of justice have to be met, without exception whatsoever, by all of man and creature. Including by Himself!" He can have no respect of persons. Mankind, since Adam and Eve the first parents created, have acquired through sinning constantly a curse on all mankind everywhere. It is written in sacred script: "The wages of sin are death!" Through His supernatural and unlimited power, God came down from Heaven, His spiritual domain, and became a flesh and blood man (Jesus Christ) to fulfill the demands of justice concerning mankind's sins. According to His predestination disposition, His Hebrew nation, in utter ignorance of what they were doing when they crucified Him, killed their own God. They wouldn't believe Him that He came on earth to save them from their sins. Because this intellectual or Being (Jesus Christ) was by nature infinitely supernatural, His body and blood bore the wrath of the offended God. His propitiation (took the place of) sacrifice of being crucified on a cross satisfied the demands of justice concerning sins (offenses against God), a universal statute forever. With the 'demands of justice' met, all mankind's members need to do to enter Paradise when they die is "Repent, be baptised in Jesus Christ's name, and endure in the faith until the end"!

7. What will happen to the earth and mankind and creature at some point in our Creator's regulated timing?

Our Lord God and Creator has promised His servants, prophets, angels, and all His saints that His creation's timing, according to ecclesiastical prudence and ultimate causal fulfillment, will be only 7,000 years long. Then at that point in time, the preparation and rearing of mankind on mother earth will no longer be carried on or needed anymore. The children of men will enter paradise, those that are worthy, and the physical material earth and universe will no longer have a cause to exist, and will be finished. "And will be rolled up like a scroll, and amidst fire and violence will cease to exist."

A new heavens and earth, called in Christian scripture "New Jerusalem" will come down from the heavens with our Creator encompassed, thereat and therein, for the children of men who are worthy to enter. Our Creator's holy City and Temple will be a spiritual paradise for the elect perpetually forever.

The reason for God's Creation is fulfilled, and all is well, very, very well!

*(Except for the unrepentant wicked, who will go off into perdition never to be heard from again!)

8. What are just some of the gifts and pleasures God's Saints will experience in paradise?

With the end of the physical and material universe, 'time', as mankind and creature apportion it, will end. No more boredom, no more tiredness brought on by work or age. No more work for food or shelter. Forever young. No more old or crippled or sick. Endless happiness and contentment. Deep fulfilling love with one's personal God, Jesus Christ. And comfort of knowing that this is your eternal, everlasting home. And forever knowing that your personal God and Father is "Jesus Christ", the Son of God, our Creator and Maker, Savior, Redeemer, Messiah, and of course, the "King of Kings"!

The Big Bang Theory

Super Nova Explosion, Universe, Big Bang

Certain people's state and claim, even though they know it is a fabrication, or even a bare-faced lie, that the physical universe and everything in it came about by a giant universal blast or explosion, many billions of years ago, of a ball of matter supposedly centered in the middle of the universe. They leave out the questions of:

1. Where did this ball of matter come from?
2. Where in the universe was this ball of matter located? Since there is no doubt that the universe is infinite and has no outer edges, how could this ball of matter find a central point from which to exist?
3. How can anyone possessing mental sanity possibly believe, that our physical universe with a zillion trillion, and infinitely more, of galaxies, stars and planets, could come

about in perfect unison and immaculate precision, in a perfectly balanced creation that now exists from a random, haphazard and extremely violent explosion?

4. If one could create a straight line, infinitely and perfectly straight, out into outer space from anywhere on earth, it would go on into outer space infinitely forever without end. There would be no end or outer edge for the straight line to end. And what they claim is that there is an outer edge, just ask yourself what is beyond that outer edge of the universe. Just an infinite amount of absolute nothingness, the same absolute nothingness that surrounds our earth which we humans refer to as space!

I ask each one of you, what would be the motive or purpose for these people to advocate a 'Big Bang Theory', if not to demoralize the about eight or nine billion human souls alive on God's green earth today? And to convince the masses of the nations on earth to advocate and believe that there is no God. They imply that just 'eat, drink and be merry, for tomorrow we may die'. And to indulge all your senses to pleasures, and that there is no God, or sin, or justice, to hold them to account.

Christ help us all!

Omnipresence And Omnipotence

1. What is omnipresence?

It is to be present at all times and at all places at all locations in the physical and spiritual universe, from the smallest of atomic particles (atom, proton, neutron, etc.) to the infinite largeness of the physical and material universe! That is just one attribute of our God, 'Jesus Christ'. If you are not a believer and obedient when He soon comes, that person will be rejected into the place of the unrepentant. Some refer to this place as fiery hell, but to be more precise, I believe it is the bottomless pit of 'outer darkness'. That unbelieving individual is imprisoned there until their resurrection just before Judgment Day, when they will be allotted a final chance to repent. Then follows the Last Judgment, then the 'end of time' as it is measured, and eternal paradise forever after.

Do you not know that a person's body is the temple of Christ. That He gives you your every heartbeat and your every breathe. And by the miracle of infinite justice and mercy, He charitably and infinitely wisely, allots you your every thought and deed (accordingly based on past performance of words and deeds in your life).

If one has an inkling of wisdom and knowledge, 'please fear Christ'! One cannot even imagine, even the wisest of scholars, the horrendous amount of pain and torment that the offended omnipotent God can inflict upon one's conscious, unrepentant bodies.

'Faith' is the key to everlasting paradise. 'Unbelief' is the key to endless perdition. Obedience in a person's life to our God's commandments that He gave to mankind through the prophet Moses are mandatory to be strictly obeyed. It is openly stated in God's Word that we are all judged by our works and words, and that we are to walk the straight and narrow path of life.

As an example in my life I have had knowledge of Christ's Spirit (omnipresence) in my body for over fifty years now. And as time and tribulations have passed, in spite of my sins and shortcomings, and outright foolhardiness, I am learning daily how to perfect my soul in my God's presence. We all are called upon to learn to be perfect to endure our God's presence and gain His mercy and forgiveness of our sins. I go on day after day learning and searching scripture and trying to reach my Maker. But Jesus Christ's immaculate majesty keeps me apart at a safe distance. If I came into His presence bearing my sins, I would instantly be burned to a crisp because of my sinful character. However, His mercy always applies to those who are innocent and obedient.

2. What is omnipotence?

Can one imagine traveling in space from our earth in a straight line until you assume to reach the edge of the physical, material universe. Even travelling at a speed a trillion times the speed of light, you could travel for a quadrillion times a trillion years, and never reach the edge of the universe.

Why? Because the universe is infinite, because it has no beginning or ending. 'Impossible', no, not spiritually impossible! It is a supernatural state of existence in the absolute essence of 'reality'! And although I am lacking in a complete understanding, that totally 'Supernatural State of Being' is the root contributor to our God's, Jesus Christ's, omnipotent presence and power. It is hard to believe by many, and understood by very few, that our Creator, manifested in the flesh as the individual 'Jesus Christ', could quench the entire existence of the whole universe, by simply uttering the command. That's what omnipotence is!

So, for God's sake, and for your simple essence of life itself sake, "Fear God!". And we all have to quit toying with a sinful lifestyle. Does one really wish to be among those who are consigned to go off into perdition into the outer darkness after the 'last judgment'? Think about it! Even a lifetime of unending pain in your lifetime is infinitely better compared to being consigned to the outer darkness of perdition for ever. Endless sorrow and torment as a just reward for simply not repenting of your sinful lifestyle on earth.

Just keep the faith and believe! "Faith, Hope and Charity" says the Apostle Paul in scripture. And then one's future will be a 'never-ending paradise' after the Last Judgment of the 'Almighty'!

Mystery of God

This is a limited narrative, explaining the elusive, yet universally decreed, 'Mystery of God'!

How did our Creator certify and establish His position as deserving omnipotent King of Kings in His planned for the future 'New Jerusalem' or 'Eternal Paradise'?

At Daniel 9:24 in the Christian Holy Bible, a shortened explanation of why and how is provided:

Daniel 9:24 - "Seventy weeks are determined upon thy people and upon thy holy city, to finish the transgression, and to make an end of sins, and to make reconciliation for iniquity, and to bring in everlasting righteousness, and to seal up the vision and prophecy, and to anoint the Most Holy."

Imagine yourself in our Creator's circumstance and situation before anything existed, in dark, infinite and empty space. A complete void of anything existing, except for Himself, the one and only supernatural infinite Entity. And His desires for a cosmic epoch, called the creation, to take place over a 7,000 years time span. During this 7,000 years creation He would literally micro manage every act and deed to take place in the heavens and earth.

For about 6,000 years now our Creator has been working to bring into 'being' a cosmic reality called in Holy Script "New Jerusalem", or what most refer to as 'paradise'. There is yet another thousand years to go in which He is Christ the Saviour, in which He establishes His Kingdom for His saints to dwell with Him (to learn to be perfect). His 7,000 years plan is to fulfill the requirements of universal justice and of His own existence, and to fulfill all that is required of Himself and His Creation, to attain universal certification for eternity thereafter.

Take note: There is, and only will be, one creation. And in this 7,000 years cosmic epoch our Creator works universally to finish the transgression or sins, and He establishes reconciliation for iniquity, and to bring in and establish everlasting righteousness for Himself and His saints. His goal is to certify and guarantee His infinite vision (or the Creation) as a physical and material reality. And for Himself to be anointed 'the Most Holy', and to make 'New Jerusalem' (a manifestation of Himself and all

His individual Saints) a spiritual reality lasting forever. Worthy mankind and creature will dwell in paradise forever.

Beyond Both Directions from One Location

A 'point' located somewhere in the vast nothingness of the universe, where physical and material matter (atoms, protons, electrons and neutrons) don't exist. You simply cannot have any 'point' anywhere when you have no outer edges to measure from, such as from even one mere atom. It is impossible to have a center of the universe when you have no outer edges to measure from a location. By simple human reasoning, this proves infinity, which in turn proves 'supernatural' (or beyond the physical and material state of existence), and its natural state of visible existence in an infinite universe full of absolute nothingness. Alas, behold, the absolute essence of the omnipresent and omnipotent Creator, the one and only God!

It is hard to imagine the spiritual and temporal aspects of infinity in the person of one alive 'Being'. An infinitely supernatural 'Being', who humankind refers to as God, or 'Creator'.

I think it is about time that we humans solved these puzzles. Yes, scholars and professors should, all mankind should, before we destroy ourselves, mankind and creatures, and render the earth uninhabitable. We need to turn to the one and only true God to save us and the earth. Mankind needs to put a permanent end to the inherent superstitions of multiple religions and philosophies that lead and convince mankind to kill one another. To the end now, in the year 2024, that a vast multitude of the nations are in a delirium of Babylonish fornication, the end thereof being whoredoms and unprecedented wars. The wicked assume that they are at the edge of destroying all life forms on earth and rendering our earth uninhabitable. Yet our leaders blindly and willfully go on, day after day, ignoring the obvious, OR deviously planning it and carrying it out. I can state with assurance that mankind is at the very, very edge of 'nuclear conflagration', or what the very wise refer to as "Nuclear Armageddon"!

Mankind's God and Creator, no matter what religion or philosophical orientation, is thoroughly disgusted with each of our godlessness, our atheism, our whoredoms, our blasphemies and our sacrileges. But I think most of all, that our Creator has exhausted His patience of mankind who do not, and refuse to, pay heed to His 'Ten Commandments'!

Do the members of the human race not know, not realize, that our heartbeats and our every breath come from God, that our every thought and deed originate at our Creator's will. We are born on this earth and live to our death in a spiritual and physical 'state of probation'. Our Creator discovers if we as individuals, or even collectively, are inclined to do good, or to do evil.

In our individual lives we experience trials and tribulations for at least two reasons as follows:

To test how useful we would be to those in heaven, and in turn, how useful we would be to our Creator Himself, when He establishes His 1,000 years Kingdom on earth, and in Paradise after the end of time (or the end of the world as we know it). On Judgment Day we are judged according to our words and deeds, whether we have done good or evil in our sojourn on this earth, while we dwell in a misty and foggy reality of the truth that we endure daily.

The more physical suffering we endure with spiritual and physical patience and endurance while we fulfill our 'probation period', the more we grow spiritually. Also, the more just pleasures we will have earned and will experience in paradise after the last Judgment Day. Unjust suffering is the spiritual nutrition that opens the gates of heaven to let us in. The unfaithful have no reward, their end is to endure a never-ending outer darkness.

The Mystery of Iniquity

To fulfill the mandatory laws of universal spiritual jurisprudence, the 'demands of justice' must always be met! The 'mystery of iniquity' can be understood in a shortened explanation as follows:

In our Creator's planning before the initiation of His actions of creating the heavens and the earth, He had to have everything planned precisely and compellingly perfect. Other wise the creation of the heavens and earth, and all forms of life from the very first beginning, throughout, and to the very ending of the purposes of the creation, would simply fail. Or it would be impossible for our Creator's 'grand plan' of paradise to become a temporal and spiritual reality. The universal 'laws of justice', which are mandatory for any words or deeds to be judged righteously, is spiritually and temporally pre-eminent in our home, the infinite universe.

Our Creator realized that there had to be justice present in every act and deed that takes place from the first of seven creation commandments, "Let there be light!", to the end point or plan of our Creator, the "New Jerusalem" paradise. Following is the 'end of time' as mankind measures it, and then follows a spiritual accounting of time.

Our Creator thought to Himself that His personal mandate and purpose was to create a perfect paradise. But all those who would enter paradise, Himself included, could not earn the pleasures of a perfect paradise, unless everyone, including Himself, had done words, acts and deeds in their lifetime worthy of reward. Or, had suffered unjustly and experienced unjust treatment in their lifetime, and who are therefore worthy of reward.

The 'Demands of Justice' being fully orchestrated and met completely in every case.

Throughout the thoroughfare of the 7,000 years creation cosmic epoch to completely meet the demands of justice as our Creator's mandate and grand plan is fulfilled, there had to be a reality of a punishment for iniquitous deeds and acts of rebellion against Him, in the past, and now, and in the future, against everything righteous and just. Therefore, a place of punishment was also created, some refer to it as 'hell', others refer to the place as 'Hades'. I refer to it as the outer darkness (and the bottomless pit of perdition).

The righteous go to heaven when they die, not the paradise 'New Jerusalem', but to a place of rest to await their consignment to paradise after the end of time and the 'last judgment'. The unrepentant wicked, if they have suffered unjustly and extensively, those that have earned reprieve because of excessive pain and sorrow in their lifetime, also go to heaven, the 'place of rest'. A few 'poisonous' individuals are consigned to the outer darkness when they die where they will exist in perpetuity (where there is weeping and wailing and the gnashing of teeth).

The very basic 'demands of justice' are always fulfilled concerning mankind and creature. Pleasure for good words and deeds, and pain for evil acts and words. Our Creator in heaven oversees all the affairs of mankind and creature, and judges accordingly. The requirements of the basic 'demands of justice' that were, and are, and always will be, are compulsory for the 'creation epoch' to proceed and come to a very satisfactory conclusion.

The ten commandments must be obeyed in order to obtain the good graces of our Lord and Creator. As it states in the Book of Revelation in the Christian Holy Scriptures, all the individual members of mankind, all those who can understand the law of good and bad, fit into one of the seven burdens that are wisely placed by our Creator to be overcome. If one overcomes their individual burden or burdens, then it states that person will attain personal salvation, and that individual will be accepted into the eternal paradise, "New Jerusalem".

Once an individual has heard and understands the 'true' word of God, they are obligated to repent from their inordinate sinful lifestyles, and walk the straight and narrow path of righteousness the rest of their days on earth.

Jesus Christ's apostles and prophets, who are wiser than I, taught that there are three personal attributes and defining qualities required in an individual, no matter what religious or belief orientation one embraces. And these three are: "Faith, Hope and Charity!"

These basic gospel messages are there in black and white in the 'Word of God', the Christian Holy Bible. Intently and studiously holding on to the doctrine of 'faith, hope and charity' throughout one's life will get one to the 'Tree of Life', and to 'Jesus Christ's Throne in Heaven', without doubt! But we must always remember that we are called upon to endure in the faith.

Faith, Hope and Charity, and patience and endurance, and personally loving God and loving your Fellowman, will gain an individual the title 'Saint'. Of all the multiple nations, religions, languages, races and cultures on this earth, mankind's God created and loves them all, and judges them all according to their works, words and deeds, whether they have done good, or whether they have done evil.

CHAPTER 2

BELIEVING IN GOD

A Matter of Faith

In a person's life, and the good and the bad fruits of it, even to after the end thereof, that all can be brought to the basics of it, that every word and deed is judged to be a matter of 'faith', and the 'expressions of belief'. Faith in a just, righteous, perfect and all-powerful God. And continuing to 'walk the path of God' (that is to love God and your fellowman) in one's life until one dies is necessary to attain life everlasting in paradise.

If a person diverts, wanders or deviates from this 'path' of God, during one's lifetime while on earth, and dies in a strange and foreign 'path', contrary to the requirements of our universal justice, then that individual has failed the state and condition of 'probation' that all the mature children of mankind must pass to qualify to enter eternal 'paradise'.

There exists a multitude of deviant obsessions and careless temptations to tempt a human soul from entering and maintaining one's faith in God. But each and every temptation in one's lifetime can be summed up (as the wise King Solomon in scripture declares): "Vanity of vanities, all is vanity!"

Just believe, all each of us have to do is 'just believe', and say and act accordingly. That's the God given formula to pass the test of 'probation' to which we are all subject.

All of us are sinners, myself included, but I have always believed in God since a young child. At present I am almost 80 years old, in October, 2024, and I have studied and treasured the 'word of God' since I first read it from cover to cover. The Christian Bible has been my source and basis of sanity in this world of multi-oriented, spiritual, physical and material, supernaturally applied consensus that the human brain is subject to, all diligently applied to my soul and consciousness. All these, by the fact that I am an 'alive being'. Just as each and everyone of you are an 'alive being', by the very nature of being a living and thinking 'electro-chemical organism' called the human person.

Almost every day negative things happen in a human life that tries to convince our brain to think: "There is no God. How can a God allow iniquity to happen? And concerns such as evolution, dinosaurs, vastness of the universe, abortion, euthanasia, and aliens, and a multitude more of negative factors that steal our faith in the existence of a righteous, just and perfect Creator."

Just take the 'jump of faith' and become a believer, and then continue down the 'path of God' that He has chosen for you. Then the Good Lord's Spirit will enlighten you with knowledge and wisdom to understand His mysteries and truths of the 'human life form'. Some individuals may even exhibit exemplified faith to the point of gaining God's gift of understanding 'hidden and secret knowledge' and 'hidden and secret wisdom', even to the point of understanding the 'Mystery of God' in its completeness.

Just be a believer in God, and He will place in your psychological make up a fear to offend Him, so through obedience one will grow in faith. Then one will start to 'love' one's true God (the most important of all His commandments).

Just believe this: "That our Creator wants each and everyone of us to be with Him in paradise. He promises to do all He can to help us climb the ladder of life to overcome sin, and to prove worthy of 'eternal paradise'. It is a spiritual imperative that we have to attain worthiness to enter into His presence."

Our God possesses infinite, immaculate majesty, and absolutely no individual can enter His presence without being burned to a crisp. Only through the manifestation of His presence in the flesh of our Lord and Savior, and our only true God "Jesus Christ", can we endure His presence and join Him in paradise.

Our God, manifested in the form of the man 'Jesus Christ', took on himself all the sins of the world, without exception to infinity, to pay the penalty of mankind's sins. He has the ultimate power to forgive our sins according to our diligence in obeying Him. If a person endures in faith and belief, Christ can wipe out and cleanse us of our sins. Jesus can make an individual worthy to enter His presence and live with Him forever in eternal paradise.

As it is stated and written in Holy Script, 'we are judged by our God according to our works and words' throughout our lifetime.

It is impossible to prove that there is no God, just look up at the infinity of the universe, and the perfection of supernatural infinity. Only the proven and absolute fool will assume it all happened, and happens by chance.

There is always a perfectly reasonable and complete explanation of all doubts concerning negative assumptions about our Creator. A person can and will experience these opposing factors in one's lifetime. But the key that opens the door to 'pure faith' is just believing.

It is all a 'matter of faith'.

Motivation for Creation

When our Creator was alone in the completely empty universe, He thought upon His future. He had always been in existence alone forever, without beginning or ending, as time as mankind measures it didn't exist yet. Our Creator (Jesus Christ) was a living 'Being' and possessed infinity and eternity as attributes. And He was conscious of His own solitude existence. In sacred writings He is referred to as God, or Creator.

As Jesus Christ, which ancient Hebrew writers referred to His name 'Jehovah', our omnipotent and omnipresent Creator, dwelt in infinite and totally dark solitude. And He was clothed with the oneness of infinity within the realms of consciousness and self awareness. And He uttered the thought "Let there be Light". And behold, spiritual light beamed throughout the infinite universe from His sacred dwelling of the infinite universe. The absolute oneness of His existence was now bathed in manifest spiritual wisdom and knowledge multiplied.

We read in Holy Script that our Creator (Jesus Christ) went on to finish the six more days of the creation account, the last creation day being a day of rest.

And as Jesus went on pondering His thoughts, He conceived of improving His lot in His lonely existence. His goal and mandate He established to be an ultimate 'Paradise', after all is said and done, to be populated with Himself as Eternal King, and with all the worthy saints and creatures from the earth earned during their days of probation on the physical earth. This perfect paradise was named by our Creator, "New Jerusalem"!

From the first day that mankind began dwelling on this earth, our Creator guides mankind and creature, to the end that, if possible, all would be worthy to enter His planned perfect paradise. After which, as mankind measures it, 'time' will end. Eternity will begin, and will go on forever without end.

We children of mankind need but to 'believe and obey' during our days of 'probation' on this earth, and we will be accepted into our Creator's Holy City and Temple, "New Jerusalem" after the 'last judgment'.

Of the 7,000 years creation event, we are presently at the door of entering the final 1,000 years. That is, the 1,000 years of our Creator's reign, or called 'Christ's Kingdom'. Will we enter 'peacefully', or at 'war'?

The Holy Bible

Open Bible

This book reveals the mind of God, the state of man, the way of salvation, the doom of sinners, and the happiness of believers.

Its doctrines are holy, its precepts are binding, its histories are true, and its decisions are immutable.

Read it to be wise, believe it to be safe, and practice it to be holy. It contains light to direct you, food to support you, and comfort to cheer you.

It is the travelers map, the pilgrim's staff, the pilot's compass, the soldier's sword, and the Christian's charter. Here, too, heaven is opened, and the gates of hell disclosed.

Christ is its grand subject, our good, its design, and the glory of God its end.

It should fill the memory, rule the heart, guide the feet. Read it slowly, frequently, prayerfully. It is a mine of wealth, a paradise of glory, and a river of pleasure.

It is given you in life, will be opened at the judgment, and be remembered forever. It involves highest responsibility, will reward the greatest labour, and will condemn all who trifle with its sacred contents.

Owned, it is riches; studied, it is wisdom; trusted, it is salvation; loved, it is character; and obeyed, it is power.

The Trinity

The trinity doctrine is taught by many Christian religious authorities. They profess in the one God, three persons doctrine. Following is my explanation of the true doctrine of one Sovereign Creator, who consists and exists, of just one Lord, one God, and only just 'one Person'.

Our eternal God is just one person by spiritual recognition and physical appearance. And by universal apportioning by spiritual infinite estate (the state of His Being in an infinite universe), this one person or one God has by natural environment omnipotence and omnipresence. And possesses other natural infinite elements or attributes existing in a spiritually infinite universal 'Entity', called and recognized by most as our 'Creator'.

This infinite Being is referred to as the Father because He created, or you could say, begot at the beginning all that exists. Our

Creator, or Father, has a body in the person of Jesus Christ, who was born of the virgin Mary by the Holy Ghost, or the miraculous power of God (referred to as the Father). His essence and projected power derived from His infinite supernatural estate in the infinite universal environment in which He existed as One Person.

When the virgin Mary gave birth to Jesus Christ, created and born of the Creator, He was therefore called the Son of God. His natural father was Himself, the Eternal God, and the Father's manifestation in the flesh was, and is, the Son of God, or the physical person 'Jesus Christ'. This miraculous conception infinitely gave a body, a physical body, to the one and only personal God and Father and Creator, 'Jesus Christ'!

According to the New Testament in the Holy Bible in the Gospel Accounts, Jesus taught His disciples and followers that "He and the Father are One!" Not two persons, but one. The flesh co-existing with and of the Father. And with the father's eternal supernatural infinite existence, explained and referred to as the 'Holy Ghost' or the 'Holy Spirit' of the one person of God, 'Jesus Christ'.

The Father and the Son and the Holy Spirit are not three individual persons manifested in one sovereign godhead. They are three distinguishing features, or names given, to one Lord, one God, and only one Person. This one person precisely manifests Himself to those who understand and believe as one infinite God and person named 'Jesus Christ'. He is the Son of God, our eternal Creator, and the Father of all that exists in the heavens and the earth.

In the name of the 'Father and the Son and the Holy Ghost', which is one Eternal Sovereign Creator of all that is, I declare and profess that "Jesus Christ" is our God and Creator!

Religions and Prophecy

Following are lists of why the world is the way it is at present:

- Many biblical prophecies are being fulfilled and in actuality there exists severe lack of faith in God.
- The nations are definitely in the 'last days', or 'end times' as mentioned prophetically in Holy Script.

- There exists at present among the nations many different religious cults.
- Atheism replacing faith in God is quite common.
- False multiple religions exist in practically all nations.

- Almost all officials everywhere declare the 'Big Bang Theory' to explain the existence of the universe.
- Most schools everywhere lack in teaching genuine moral values.
- Most schools teach evolution of species, instead of God's Creation account of Adam and Eve.

- Blasphemy and sacrilege committed on a daily basis by many, including most leaders and rulers among the peoples.
- There exists a shortage of integrity among the priesthood.
- Godliness in most nations has been replaced by the doctrine and lifestyle of 'eat, drink and be merry, for tomorrow we die!'

- The teaching and obedience of our God's 'ten commandments' are ignored practically everywhere.
- Israel's plans to build a temple in Jerusalem displacing the Muslim temple causes grief among the about two billion Muslims in the world.

- Mankind in general, although most don't believe or understand, get all their thoughts and deeds from our Creator, 'Jesus Christ'. Our God diligently follows a 'plan of salvation' to gain access to heaven for as many as possible who are worthy, and who have earned their salvation. Freewill among mankind prevails, and we receive our just desserts!

CHAPTER 3

PERSONAL PROPOSITIONS

Joy and Happiness Beyond Understanding

Bride embracing her Grandmother after Wedding Ceremony

Imagine yourself in a situation that you are going for a walk with Jesus Christ, (the manifestation in the flesh of the Eternal Creator) and you are holding His hand and walking together along a path in paradise. Butterflies, flowers and birds are everywhere around you and Jesus, and a herd of antelope with their young are feasting on pure and lush green grass nearby. Your Lord and Saviour asks you quietly: "Do you love Me?" Your heart starts pounding as your lips utter sweet and delightful words: "You are my heart and soul, my love, how can I not love You?" And you soon ask: "Please grant me Father, that my joy and happiness will be full?" And your Lord says: "What is your request my child?" You ask: "Please grant me that I might have permission to bow down before You and worship You forever, then my joy and happiness will be full to overflowing?" Christ answers: "Yes, my child, you may have your request" and then adds: "There are differing ways to express your love and devotion to Me. Such as loving and serving your fellowman, your brothers and sisters who abide in My love." You look in your Lord's eyes as He smiles and says: "I love you, my child, and I will grant you everlasting paradise." He adds: "You and all my saints, your loving brothers and sisters, will dwell for eternity with Me in My eternal Temple and City in heavenly paradise, prepared for those who are worthy to enjoy never ending joy and happiness forever." You ask Jesus as you continue down the sunshiny path: "Please make me to love You and serve You forever, my Lord, my heart is swollen with love!"

Through the Wisdom of God, "New Jerusalem" is Created

The scriptures quoted below are from: Luke 13:18, 19, 20, 21. And Daniel 9:24.

Luke 13: 18 – Then said He, Unto what is the Kingdom of God Like? And whereunto shall I resemble it?

Luke 13:19 – It Is like a grain of mustard seed, which a man took, and cast into his garden; and it grew, and waxed a great tree; and the fowls of the air lodged in the branches of it.

Luke 13:20 – And again He said, whereunto shall I liken the kingdom of God?

Luke 13:21 – It is like leaven, which a woman took and hid in three measures of meal, till the whole was leavened.

Daniel 9:24 – Seventy weeks are determined upon thy people and upon thy holy city, to finish the transgression, and to make an end of sins, and to make reconciliation for iniquity, and to bring in everlasting righteousness, and to seal up the vision and prophecy, and to anoint the Most Holy.

The creation of the universe and mankind was started about 6,000 years ago, with the end purpose of spiritually and physically producing, or manufacturing, and manipulating mankind and all earthly events, or to bring to be, or to create the reality of, a perfect paradise at the completion of 7,000 years (called in Holy Script "New Jerusalem"). A forever spiritual and physical union of God's grace and forever after for worthy, believing members of mankind.

The creation of the heavens and earth, and mankind and creatures, can be likened to a factory manufacturing items, small and great, to be of use to God and Mankind.

Our Creator, in His infinite wisdom, spiritually manufactured and produced the physical universe, with one particular part or item, the earth, to be of imperative importance to do with His

Grand Plan. His earth was and is the factory for mankind to use for our spiritual benefit. Dwelling with our Creator's Holy Spirit within us, He guides and directs us through our free will to choose to do good or evil. To the end that only believers and the righteous could receive occupancy in the future paradise of God.

It is of necessity that we individuals attain spiritual growth along with our physical essence during our 'days of probation' while on this earth. Non-believers and the unrepentant wicked at their death cannot ever enter Christ's 1,000 years Kingdom on earth. This is immediately followed by the appearance of our Creator's spiritual city, the heavenly paradise called "New Jerusalem". This eternal Paradise is based and manufactured from a foundation of physical and spiritual activities of good or bad by mankind committed in the flesh.

I don't think that there is any member of mankind that will ever be able to fully comprehend and understand the infinite attributes, qualities and orientations of our infinite God 'Jesus Christ'. Mankind is therefore called upon by necessity to practice and display faith while they live in their days of 'probation' on earth. 'Belief' is the key that opens the door to enter the paradise of God.

Mankind is almost at the 6,000 years mark since the creation started, and will be followed by the 1,000 years reign of Christ's Kingdom on this earth. The completion of which will be the end of the physical universe, immediately followed by the 'Last Judgment', then the new beginning of the kingdom of God, the eternal city and temple called "New Jerusalem". This 'entity' is a supernatural manifestation of our Creator and His Saints after the end of time. Believers will dwell with their heavenly Creator in perpetual bliss forever!

Beautiful Rainbow

Beautiful Evening Sunset After Rain

The first thing that a person should realize is that our God is a pleasant and friendly person. He possesses all the good virtues and is a goodly person to know by young and old alike. He is like a beautiful rainbow up in the sky, as if a lovely smile from a wonderful guy. His sign of a rainbow shows that it has rained and watered the earth, proclaiming peace to mankind forever. He is a God of love who offers His hand, requesting to obey His laws to prosper and thrive.

But many of us prefer sin, determined to go our own way. Indulging in pleasures that are not worth much, we enjoy for a moment the forbidden fruit. Thereby offending our God who withdraws beyond our reach, but offers to forgive our sins if we will believe in Him and teach.

The heavens and earth and all that is therein were all created by God by His uttering a simple thought. He also created peace and rest for the weary souls who believe in Him and His goodness.

The birds and the bees enjoy the sun shining brightly, and the smile of a child, all trusting God rightly. The Prince of Peace ruling, and protecting all His saints and believers, will surely come very quickly. Look up and see God coming in His majesty and might, knowing that the harvest has come, and that believing in Christ is right.

Always remember that beautiful rainbow up in the sky, as a loving smile from a wonderful guy.

A Whistle and a Tweet

Although life can be gloomy and very disappointing at times, even harsh and unforgiving, our God will never let us down. He will never betray us, and assuredly He will lead all His saints to a very bright and cheery future.

Let's imagine that I'm a bird in distress, and it's a very dark and gloomy day. I am hunted and lost, and the evil so depressing that I can't imagine that tomorrow will be better. The dark reality of the situation has left me with nothing but sorrow. To my God I ask that He take me up and away from this anguish and this pain, hoping that I am not insane.

I feel that I am a black and hollow ghost, that Christ's light has left me. Near the edge of the deadly host, the devil's bite I feel. From my strangled spirit I cry, no one understands my doom. All my life is a burden to pay a ransom for my body to nurture and sustain. My feathers have lost their lustre and I can no longer fly. Wit and humour have abandoned me, I just wish the sky would be blue. My will to live in the confusion has left me, the plague will not go away. I have a desire to fly but my body is too heavy to heft. I look up and see a twinkling star which reminds me of the day. If only I could get over this curse in my life that is laid out before me as on a tray.

As if my eyes are tightly shut when I look around to see, but my heart is all surrounded by bright gold. Alas, could I be a little wise? I'll sing a song and cheer as I did not lose my life. Hooray, I am still here, and beat this mad confusion and strife. The gloomy bird I used to be is now as a sweet-smelling flower, forever singing a happy song with 'a whistle and a tweet'.

Envelope all Truth

In writing this book I have tried to relate to my readers, and explain many truths and mysteries. I have tried to reveal the 'Mystery of God' in its fullness as I understand and perceive it, and as the concept is understood in it's true reality. Although this book is lacking in its presentation and style, I believe the reader will gain a greater understanding of 'the way true reality is in this life', to his or her benefit.

I believe that our Lord wishes His people to know and understand the length and width and height in its fulness, of all the universe and creation. But to know and understand infinity in its completeness may always be beyond humanities grasp. But to perceive the Holy Ghost (the Spirit of God) in our daily affairs on earth is truly a gift indeed.

I have dwelt and focused my attention for many decades to understand the 'Mystery of God' in its fulness. Observing that most people are lacking in the spirit of listening and heeding, I write and on occasion I speak about the imperative to 'repent from our selfish ways, and be baptized in Jesus Christ's name, and for us to endure in the true faith forever'. It is the simple gospel message that has been shared and preached by many for almost 2,000 years.

Be it far from me to pretend that I know and understand all the facts and realities. But I have perceived and know through faith in our Lord and Saviour that I must share and preach the knowledge and wisdom that I do possess, not only to help my fellowman, but it is necessary to achieve my own personal salvation also.

It would be a divine gift indeed to know and understand all things, and the 'spirit of truth' is written and promised to come and appear to all peoples and nations in these indeed, last days. The reality in its fulness of infinity I have tried to understand. But the universe in its vastness is probably beyond mankind's intellect to grasp and comprehend. Yet we can look up at night and witness and know that, yes, it is vast and it is a reality to accept. The 'big bang theory' as to the universe's existence is nothing but like a little child's understanding. If one could travel in a perfectly straight line away from the earth forever, one would never ever come to the outer edge of the physical, material universe. If there exists an outer rim to the universe and God's creation, it is only empty space beyond that, forever for eternity. The very same empty space that is beyond earth's atmosphere.

On occasion the question arises: "When and where did time start?" I would suggest that time, as mankind measures it, started at about the moment our Creator commanded: "Let there be light!" I presume that time, as it is measured and observed, will cease to exist when the heavens and earth as we perceive them disappear. Followed immediately after by the paradise of God, called in sacred script "New Jerusalem", and becomes a spiritually and physically perceived reality.

To envelope all truth and reality and contain it all in a single thought process is probably only achieved and comprehended in its fulness by our Creator Himself. After the end of time as measured by mankind on earth is accomplished, our Creator will bring all acts of man and creature to the 'Last Judgment Day'. Thereafter only the righteous believers will be received into eternal paradise, time (spiritually) will follow without end!

Before and After

To achieve the goals of His creation, our Creator in His infinite wisdom and knowledge decided that there had to exist a physical and material universe to co-exist within the supernatural heavens (the infinite universe) in which He dwells. Since by supernatural reality (possessing infinity), He possessed omnipresence and omnipotence, and He proceeded to create the heavens and the earth. His created earth was to be the dwelling place for all mankind and creatures, where they would all live out their 'days of probation'.

In our Creator's infinite wisdom and knowledge, He decreed and commanded that all the members of mankind must work out their eternal salvation, or the opposite, their eternal damnation. For reward or punishment, according to acts and deeds of good or bad, to justly and righteously prevail, the divine 'Demands of Justice' must be met and forever maintained.

The universe, an infinite, previously empty space, has no outer edge. We can presume then that the universe can have no center by theory (yet the earth indeed exists in a particular time and space). The natural reality of this absolute is that we exist only in an environment of supernatural and naturally acquired essence. All creation is thoroughly maintained and administered by an eternal 'Being', who we call our God and Creator.

By physical nature, the trials and tribulations for all the members of mankind are universal, experienced to one degree or another, or in one manner or another, by every single person. The main beacon of God's 'plan of creation' was to save mankind from there sins (because we all sin), so that in the end of His creation He could share His home, the Eternal Paradise, with those who passed the test of 'probation' while living on this earth. We are all called upon to overcome, and prevail in life. Our God created a concept and reality, of a Saviour and Redeemer for all mankind, according to their belief in Him. And He assumed the supreme role Himself, according to His Grand Plan of creating the heavens and the earth (there is only one infinite eternal God, and absolutely no room or position for any other).

In the person of the eternal God in the flesh (Jesus Christ), about 2,000 years ago He suffered and died on a cross. He took upon Himself, and endured all the punishments that were due sinners who passed the test of 'probation' and were worthy of forgiveness. The unrepentant stand rejected. Our Creator had and has a 'plan' and a Universal Supernatural 'Vision', which undeniably exists as a reality. The 'Demands of Justice' will be met, so we all must learn to listen to and obey our Creator. In the end, the righteous will receive the eternal reward of everlasting life in Paradise!

My Proposal to God

You are my Lord and my God,
You are my Creator and Father,
You are like unto a husband and lover,
My companion Lord Jesus Christ.

You walk with me wherever I go,
You lead me up the straight and narrow path,
Your Spirit dances with me all the day long,
My every thought You create in my heart.

You cherish me with infinite love,
You warm me when I feel cold,
You lift me from hell's abyss,
My soul longs to behold my Lord.

You grant me my faith and my hope,
You bless me with a desire for You,
Your love for me lifts my spirit,
My heart leaps for joy at Your call.

You are my Light and my Life,
You are a window to my soul,
You are the only 'Being' that gives love,
My body and spirit thrive at your command.

You have compassion on me when I fall short,
You forgive me and blot out all my sins,
You are my Saviour that I thank,
My heart bursts with my love for You.

You save me from all the world's harms,
You grant me to overcome evil,
Your love for me hides Your wrath,
My salvation lies only in Your hands.

You are the high and holy God,
You created the heavens and the earth,
You are the infinite and omnipotent Judge,
My Master and Saviour Jesus Christ.

You make me to fall down before You,
You guide me down the path to Your Throne,
Your presence I feel throughout my body,
My footsteps through my life shout Your name.

Jesus Christ you're like unto a Husband and Lover,
Your many blessings shield me from the heat of the day,
I propose to You and offer You my heart and soul,
I surely love you my Lord and my God!

CHAPTER 4

GOD AND MAN IN ACTION

Random Thoughts Regarding God in Action

At Present, the world of mankind is on the brink of World War 3, or Nuclear Armageddon, in total fulfillment of biblical prophesies.

Every Hebrew and Christian biblical prophecy concerning these 'last days' or 'end of times' is in the very process of being fulfilled. Our Creator, Jesus Christ, symbolically walks up and down the surface of the earth of mankind and creature, bringing to pass His Grand Plans and Ordinances. We are just at the edge of the 6,000 years of creation, and extremely soon we will be entering the beginning of the 7,000 years of the creation epoch, or at the doorstep of the 1,000 years of Christ's Kingdom.

Our Creator's 'Plan of Salvation' will be fulfilled without spiritual or temporal error. The repentant righteous will end up in eternal paradise, whereas the unrepentant wicked will end up in that 'outer darkness' that was prepared for them. The wicked endorsement of the 'Babylonian Whore' (which can be understood as gross sexual whoredoms) has and will bring about their downfall. This 'whore' corrupts the hearts of the unfaithful to indulge in explicit and immoral sexual practices, contrary to the morals of the just and righteous. Wickedness, iniquity, abomination, blasphemy and sacrilege, and especially gross sexual whoredoms (which can be symbolic and described by the single term, 'Babylon'). It states in sacred script that Babylon will fall in one hour.

Note: An all-out nuclear weapon exchange on our earth between those nations possessing nuclear weapons would result in the destruction of all nations, and it would take about one hour to fully destroy the 'Plan of God' and 'ruin the earth' of all life, or so the wicked think. But it is beyond the wicked to perceive that 'Armageddon' is the war of the Almighty, and His omnipotent hands and means will bring it to fully take place. The destruction will take place at the hands of the Almighty, and the repentant righteous will survive (about a tenth of the total population of the earth will survive) and will witness the soon after First Resurrection.

Sin and whoredoms has brought the wrath of the offended Creator to act on behave of His saints. It states in scripture that the unrepentant will be destroyed, and the earth will blossom thereafter in complete peace and rest in Christ's 1,000 years Kingdom.

Illicit and explicit sexual words and deeds has and will in the very near future bring upon a mostly unexpecting population a nuclear holocaust. In the Christian Holy Bible this fire and destruction is referred to in the Book of Revelation as "Armageddon".

There is no solution, delaying or cancelling or preventing of Armageddon, but the 'saints' always have the hope of a peaceful transition into 'Christ's Kingdom'. The nations of mankind have been led on to this point of time on earth, and because of severe unrepentance on the part of all nations, the 'Good Lord' will carry out His plans to complete fulfilment. Six thousand years of iniquity among the nations has brought this terrible event on earth to a point where now it is too late to stop its progression to fulfillment. My advice is: 'Call on the name of the Lord asking to be spared'. You may be blessed and spared a death of fire and total destruction.

Acts of treason and theatres of war at Present: Middle East wars, Israel, Hamas, Hezbollah, Lebanon, Iran, Houthi's; a war between NATO funded Ukraine and victim Russia and supporters; Muslim versus Jewish peoples; the Western Alliance countries (mostly NATO members) – United States and European nations – against the Eastern alliance (Russia, China, Iran, North Korea; BRICS and SCO nations united in economic, security and military affairs.

United States, NATO, Japan, South Korea, Taiwan, New Zealand, and Australia against India and China and Asian allies plus Russia. The south China sea is a tinder box of fire to cause an explosion of violence in and throughout Asia and the Pacific Ocean regions.

Ukraine versus Russia. Ukraine is a proxy nation that NATO countries use to try and destroy Russia. NATO leaders should stop and consider that if Russia decided to pre-emptively attack the United States and NATO with nuclear weapons, Russia could literally turn the United States and Canada, and Europe to complete fire and ashes within an hour or two. That is Nuclear Armageddon in Reality and all the nations on earth would be involved and turned into ashes and gigantic piles of rubble. In a very short period of time.

Soldiers and civilians are being killed and wounded every single day already. The United States and the leaders of NATO countries (European) want to place missiles on the border with Russia in Ukraine in particular.

Note: A hypersonic nuclear missile could hit the Russian capital Moscow in three or four minutes or less. This could decapitate the Russian government and all their leadership with just one nuclear missile. Russia is fighting back to prevent this from happening, and invaded Ukraine to prevent (NATO) nuclear missiles from being deployed anywhere that close in any neighboring country. NATO has already crossed several red lines that Russia has warned against, and NATO, through proxy Ukraine, is aggressively pushing military provocations against Russia. F-16 fighter jets are now deployed against Russia, and Ukraine is intent on flying these nuclear capable bombers as soon as they possibly can to bomb and destroy Russian targets. NATO nations are considering allowing long range missiles to blow up targets far into the interior of Russia. If this happens, it may be the last 'red line' crossed before full-on nuclear war erupts globally!

These human beings of the western NATO nations are acting nothing less than devils, demons in human flesh. They are devilish perverts in mind and body. They are acting in ways that mimic how Satan's demons would act – 'to destroy the Plan of God' and 'to ruin the earth' and make it uninhabitable by any life forms.

Just watch and listen to many of these leaders and rulers of the peoples. I can not see or imagine where they do not know what they are doing as their words and actions betray and reveal their stance and plans. I cannot help but judge them according to their blindness in their fervor to lead the nations to their total destruction. These supposedly worthy leaders have to know what the consequences of an all-out nuclear exchange would do to mankind and creature on this planet – and they blindly and vainly carry on anyway, celebrating their iniquitous words and deeds.

Is this not a 'demonic interlude' before all-out war happens. And why would our Creator bring about such a tragic circumstance for mankind to face at this time? Because the masses of mankind on the earth at present, have utterly failed to repent from carrying on in their life of pagan acts and deeds, in particular 'whorish' acts and deeds. And because the masses have failed to acknowledge and obey their God's commandments.

Our Creator's Love Prevails

In the first place, paradise (heaven) would fail to be paradise with any rebels present. All of our Creator's works in His creation is to accomplish the righteous and just paradise in the end, to last for an eternity thereafter. Christ had to wisely create a system in which man and creature could work out their salvation and earn for themselves to be accepted into everlasting paradise after the end of time. A 'system' where the unrepentant rebels could be justly contemned.

Christ created the heavens and the earth, and our first parents Adam and Eve, about 6,000 years ago. Our God is omnipotent and omnipresent, and He is an invisible, supernatural and infinite Spirit. His priority is to protect the righteous and just saints by weeding out the unrepentant wicked and rebellious, who are trouble-makers, so that they cannot enter paradise and spoil everything for everyone.

Yet He is ready, willing and able to share His love and forgiveness, His greatest attributes, with all the repentant and obedient among all the nations, cultures, races, languages and peoples of mankind. Christ's justice and righteousness is perfect, and we all are judged according to our works (and all incapable of sin such as babies and children, and those who are mentally incompetent are accepted), that we as individuals commit while we are alive on the earth.

And we receive from our God and Judge pleasure and pain as allotted while on this earth according to our works, with our eternal salvation in paradise being the goal. Such as: It amounts to how much pain and suffering we endure during our lifetime on earth decides the question of how many pleasures and blessings we beautifully experience in everlasting paradise. The opposite, I am sure, for the unrepentant wicked who don't experience pain and suffering, and overly indulge in pleasures and sin, as they dwell on earth.

Our Creator, Jesus Christ's cause, is infinitely righteous and just, and 'He does not make mistakes' under any circumstances. We all get exactly what we deserve, keeping in mind that 'paradise' is the goal sought after.

Throughout Christ's creation of 7,000 years (we are right at the edge of the 6,000 years point) truth and justice and His victory is assured. Although some individuals will try to contemn God's system or enrollment into paradise, and will accuse Him of lack of justice and lack of love.

But our God and Creator, Jesus Christ, is abounding in 'love'. He has established a place of 'pleasurable abode' to shield believers from all the cruel darts of the unrepentant wicked. 'Love' is Jesus Christ's key attribute that He bountifully shares and allots to those who are worthy and diligently seeking for it.

Free Will

The living human body is an electro-chemical organism. It's health and intellect being dependant on food, water and shelter. With these ingredients, our thinking capacity is totally independent of outer control or manipulation. We are completely free to make decisions and commit actions of right or wrong under normal circumstances. There are exceptions to this rule, such as being under the influence of alcohol, drugs, or for example, being manipulated by lies and propaganda.

According to sacred script, our first parents Adam and Eve fathered humanity. We humans inherited from them all our physical and mental attributes. They also handed down to all future generations of mankind the attribute, or gift, of 'free will'. We can freely make decisions to act, or not to act, to say or not to say, in different circumstances according to our accumulated knowledge and experience, and acquired mentality and intellect.

We are entirely 'free agents', and physical and mental beings with 'free will' intellect!

Atheists would probably agree with this assessment.

As an individual with somewhat spiritual contact with my God, I contemplate and add the spiritual dimension. Normally within our bodies we are free to sin or do evil, or to do good. Upon such actions we accumulate virtues or vices in our mental makeup and our spiritual being, which can become habit forming in our character analysis. The 'God factor' becomes imminent.

For example, if we choose to do something evil, our God's judgments take effect on our spiritual souls, and translate into our physical and mental bodies to eventually acquire evil personalities. Without repentance by that personality, or individual, or complete change of heart in their lifetime on earth, they stand rejected by our God and Judge, Jesus Christ. There are a few individuals who have deliberately committed so much wickedness that they are determined as being 'past repentance'!

Psychiatrists and psychologists would likely follow my reasoning and agree somewhat, but would add that this is the precise outcome of the human species, even without God's intervention. I implore readers and hearers, do not tempt fate by continuing down a path of wicked works and words. Under no circumstances in this earthly dimension can an individual cheat or escape justice. Our Creator made and fashioned the human creature with all outcomes and circumstances applied perfectly, and justly in place!

If an individual struggles without stop against Christ and His saints, and his peoples on earth, then that person, or those persons, will be consigned to an eternal damnation, justly so!

Our Lord and God, Jesus Christ, built into the human creature the capability of free will and free agent. Being omnipresent, and His Spirit dwelling in each of our hearts, He is fully aware of our every thought and deed in the outmost detail.

In His own cosmic and universal authority and detailed judgments, and in His holy perfect Majesty, He can, will, and does give all of us our every word and deed. Knowing and believing this concept and experience should not affect our belief and freewill actions.

Please do not get mentally stuck on ifs, ands and buts! Acknowledge Jesus Christ, and do not delay accepting Him as your personal Saviour and God! That is what the 'human experience' is all about. Remember that Christ is our 'light and life' source that cooperates within our will to act or speak.

Wars and Armed Conflicts

World War 2 Sniper Providing Cover for Medic Working on Wounded Soldier

Christian Holy Bible:
Amos 4:13 – "For, lo, He that formeth the mountains, and createth the wind, and declareth unto man what is his thought, that maketh the morning darkness, and treadeth upon the high places of the earth, The LORD, the God of Hosts, is His name.

- Leader's wills overshadowed by evil intentions of their own greed and lust, and vanity.
- The world and mankind are facing existential crisis at this time.
- War mongering thrives in too many nations.
- Most nations are more than willing to solve issues militarily.
- War propaganda is proliferating among far too many nations, poisoning people's minds to hate and violent acts.

- Mankind's evolutionary economic development is threatened with extinction.

- Russia's existence is threatened by the war in Ukraine.

- There exists on earth an 'existential threat' to Russia, Chinas and the United States.

- The Ukraine (NATO) Russia war is quickly leading to a conventional war between Russia and the proxy Ukraine (of the NATO/United States), which neither side will accept losing. Very soon World War 3 will begin, and quickly escalate into nuclear war, or 'Nuclear Armageddon'. Mankind's precarious political, economic, military, religious, anti-morality stand in almost all nations has brought us to the point of being just one step from 'global conflagration'.

- At present there are many global military hot spots such as: China versus Taiwan (USA); Israel/Iran; Ukraine/Russia (USA, NATO); USA military occupation of Iraq and Syria; Israel/Hamas; Israel/Hezbollah.

- The wars in Ukraine and Israel are quickly escalating to the critical mass point.

- The 'East' and the 'West' leaning nations are joining formations against one another, which will very soon lead to conventional, and evolve into determined nuclear conflict.

- There are wars, riots, revolutions, violent demonstrations worldwide.

- Terrorism is spreading worldwide.

- Both Russia and China have already won the arms race, with the western nations, in particular the USA, falling even years behind in some military technologies.

Political Turmoil

- Capitalism is threatened by socialism ideals worldwide.
- Corruption is widespread in many government organizations.
- Government policies favour the rich and powerful in practically every nation.
- Bribery and threats are widespread in most governments.
- The nations of the world are 'shipwrecked' by many generations of political malpractice.
- The world is teetering economically and financially on the precipice of oblivion.
- There is a severe lack of 'moral and proper' government globally.
- The 'World Economic Forum' and their corrupt policies and influence are weakening global health and wellbeing.
- Many diseases and pandemics are causing global and political havoc.
- There is a continuing lack of political will to face reality and the coming 'end'.
- The New World Order controversy is causing indifference among our leaders.
- Many anti-God policies globally are causing gross immorality to proliferate.

- The masses are indoctrinated and corrupted by lies and gross propaganda.
- The Israel/Palestinian problem is very near breaking point and could trigger global violence and conflagration.
- The plans of Israel to demolish the Muslim Temple Shrine in Jerusalem, and replace it with a Jewish Temple is causing major Israel/Muslim violence.

Global Concerns

- Natural disasters are taking place globally at an escalating pace.
- Climate change is causing a multitude of problems worldwide, such as floods, droughts, hurricanes.
- Suicides are increasing in practically every nation multifold.
- Illegal drugs and prostitution in every nation are causing unrest and violence.
- Genetically modified organisms are negatively affecting everything alive on our, so far, green planet.

Homelessness

Homeless Holding Cardboard

There are millions of unemployed working adults in every major country on earth.

- High unemployment in all nations breeds violence and homelessness.
- The extremely rich minorities on earth versus the poorer majorities causes social injustice and violence.
- The homeless and refugee crisis worldwide is causing violence, injustice, starvation and disease.
- There are always shortages of homes, food, clean water and energy among the poor, and poorer nations on earth.

Destiny of Mankind

Stairway to Mankind's Knowledge Made of Books

Isaiah 45:25 – "In the Lord shall all the seed of Israel be justified, and shall glory."

Is the destiny of all mankind to enter paradise eventually, sooner or later, according to each one's state of grace?

All of mankind, no matter what race, skin color, language or culture, are all born with no knowledge, and no memory to start out their life on earth. We are all born equal, and start our life on earth at conception. All of those individuals who are born lacking a healthy nature in some way, shape or form, are in a way blessed. Our common Creator owes such individuals a debt because of unjust treatments that they didn't deserve, and because they have been denied a healthy and equal start in their journey through life. It is good for any individual to be owed something from their Creator, because that is an important step towards entering paradise.

For all those who are physically and mentally healthy, if they are morally inclined to prayer and good works, no matter what race or religion, then they are step by step building up a treasure for themselves both on earth and in paradise. The 'Demands of Justice' must always be fulfilled. When and if an individual becomes aware of the true nature of our common Creator, it is expected that they will align their worship and prayers accordingly (at some point in their life before they pass away in death hopefully).

The day a human is born is the day they start the process of learning about who they are, and begin learning about their environment (their parents and caregivers). As they grow physically and mentally, an individual's five senses feed information about their environment to their memory, and the power of their natural intellect convinces them that it is the true and proper way. Those who love and care for them provide all the necessities of their life. So almost all individuals follow the traditions, cultures and customs of their parents almost automatically, which is a blessing of our God. A few of which at times can be harmful to one's relationship with one's Creator (religious or political terrorism for example).

What I am trying to explain is that all mankind could be justified to some extent or other because almost all individuals are lacking in true and honest guidance and direction from their birth to their death. We are all born in a state of ignorance as to our true destiny. By natural order and family values we are all lacking in knowledge (and wisdom) how to worship and please our Creator Jesus Christ. He is the all-knowing Creator who judges righteously and justly, and takes all things into consideration in every individual life.

It is imperative that we must remember that the 'Ten Commandments' rule, in as much as we are aware of them. They happen to also agree to the natural laws of human nature and social cohesion in mankind's societies. And we are surely judged according to our words and deeds committed in the flesh, in as much as how much evil or good was in our hearts when we committed the deed.

In one's past, having committed good or evil acts and words, could to a just degree be justified, but any future acts and words are judged according to their merit. During a person's life while on earth, there always exists the opportunity to repent from their sins and evil deeds (stop doing vain and selfish acts and words), and learn to love your God, and love your fellowman (these are our Lord's two main commandments – obey them in your life, and salvation is yours to experience forever).

For the 'demands of justice' to be pure and valid during and throughout theological and natural decree and discourse during our God's epic cosmic affair, wickedness must be punished and righteousness must be rewarded. Unfortunately, many fail to repent during their natural life on earth, and they have indeed earned their own condemnation.

CHAPTER 5

EXPANDING UNIVERSAL REASONINGS

Expanding the Intellect

Looking down as with the eyes of angels, I imagine in my heart all the goings on among the children of men. Then I look in a mirror and I do not recognize who I have become. I look deep down into my eyes to possibly view my inner self and the state of my soul. And I am blinded by the sinful darkness of my selfishness and the deceitfulness I daily practice. My inner self cries out: "Oh Lord, please save me from this hellish darkness!"

I realize that to enlighten my inner self and my spiritual soul, and to achieve intelligence and knowledge while dwelling in my days of 'probation' on this earth, then I must approach God (Jesus Christ) in humility and in a spirit of submission.

'Jesus Christ' is the 'light and the life' of the world, and of all mankind. If an individual does not acknowledge and humble oneself before 'Christ' when they have heard of Him, then that person will intellectually dwell in the darkness. They will not know and possess Christ's 'light and life' giving temporal and spiritual nutrition. It is written in holy script that they will 'dwell in the darkness'.

Following are scripture quotations from the Christian Bible:

Ecclesiastes 1:2 – "Vanity of vanities, saith the preacher, vanity of vanities; all is vanity."

Proverbs 1:7 – "The fear of the Lord is the beginning of knowledge: But fools despise wisdom and instruction."

John 1:4 – "In Him was Life, and the Life was the Light of mankind."

John 1:14 – "And the Word was made flesh and dwelt among us." (Jesus Christ is the 'Word')

Remote Control Over All God's Creation

Planet Earth Floating Between Nurturing, Protective Hands

Following are quotations from the King James version of the Christian Holy Bible:

Jeremiah 10:23 – "Oh Lord, I know that the way of man is not in himself: It is not in man that walketh to direct his steps."

Amos 4:13 – "For, lo, He that formeth the mountains, and createth the wind, and declareth unto man what is his thought, that maketh the morning darkness, and treadeth upon the high places of the earth. The Lord, the God of Hosts, is His name."

There should be no doubt in anyone's heart and mind, that we get our every thought and deed at God's direction. Don't be mistaken, we all have freewill from birth, to do good or evil. After the thought or deed are committed by an understanding individual, we are judged according to God's commandments and are laden with reward or punishment (the degree thereof according to Christ's discretion and judgment concerning the state of one's grace at that time). A lifetime of doing good works will be rewarded by Christ with blessings, whereas a lifetime of committing evil words and deeds will render no rewards of Christ, but will result in curses throughout their life. There exists always the possibility of a change of heart, and repentance can take place at any time. In our God's infinite knowledge and christening we are indeed masters of our own destiny or fate. Jesus Christ indeed carries us in His loving hands throughout our lives, and only asks that we appreciate His efforts and do our duty to acknowledge and obey Him.

Some reminders to think upon are following:

- The whole creation and everything done in it is intimately controlled by our omnipotent and omnipresent Creator.
- Jesus Christ's 'Light and Life' has presence in every single 'being' that has ever been, is now at present, and into the future for eternity.
- Christ's spiritual presence created the heavens and the earth by His almighty supernatural power (which brought physical time, as mankind knows and measures it, into existence).
- After the 'last judgment' and Christ's heavenly paradise called, "New Jerusalem" is a finished spiritual construction and brought down to earth for the righteous to enter, all the physical heavens and earth will disappear and cease existence ever again.

- Only the righteous mankind and creature, as our Creator judges each individual, will be invited into exquisite paradise to dwell with their God Forever.
- Jesus Christ's complete victory over all evil will have infinitely been achieved forevermore. And all of us who believe in Him and obey Him shall dwell in everlasting 'paradise' forever.

Believing in Justice in Injustice

Do you believe in God? Do you believe in a righteous and just God? Do you believe in a God who is omnipotent and omnipresent? And that He is infinitely perfect in everything He does. Do you believe that there is no variance whatsoever in these truths?

And if one does believe that God is none other than 'Jesus Christ' as manifested in the flesh in our world to those who are seeking true truth and perfect justice. And to all those who are honestly seeking the Creator of all the heavens and the earth (the creation of the universe), then our Savior will manifest Himself to you over time according to your diligence in practising patience and endurance.

One will not understand or comprehend all the virtuous attributes of our Creator Jesus Christ unless one practices true belief and (especially) faith, and if one is willing to humble themselves in this world of gross vainness.

Belief and faith in the unseen and unwitnessed Creator are imperative in one's search for justice, in a world where injustice seems to be universal, and in a world where evil everywhere seems to reign and prosper and have victory over righteousness. The righteous suffer for reward, whereas the wicked earn their damnation.

And yet Christ's 'Light and Life', which dwells in all God's creatures, will open the eyes and ears of all the righteous who seek and obey Him, and especially all those who believe in Him. I believe that Christ's Spirit makes His abode in my heart, as in the hearts of all those who honestly and faithfully believe in Him.

My Lord Jesus has granted me to thankfully feel and enjoy His presence from time to time throughout my adult life. He comforts me when I am low, and encourages me when I need encouragement. Each day brings a new experience to increase my faith and belief.

When the day of my death arrives, I trust and know that it will be painless and without torturous ailments. To all those unbelievers who witness what they believe to be a totally unjust and painful suffering, and possibly violent death, they will think and utter the blasphemous comment: "How can there be a God when such an unjust and merciless suffering and death reign on this earth?"

I strongly believe that Jesus Christ, upon His merciful judgment, will have concluded that I have been victorious in my days of probation on this earth, and that I have overcome all the evil influences that are common to all mankind (especially the Babylonian whoredoms).

All an individual is called upon to do is just believe and have faith in a just and righteous God, who manifested Himself in the flesh in the person of "Jesus Christ" about 2,000 years ago. And after exercising faith and belief in Him, He will reveal Himself to you through spiritual words and deeds, to your relief and pleasure and contentment.

"True justice always radiates everywhere in the universe in spite of the appearance of injustice in daily activities amongst mankind! It has been sometimes claimed that the end justifies the means, but only with the sovereign Creator 'Jesus Christ' can everything be justified!"

"Babylon" – Fornication and Illicit Pleasures

The following quotations are taken from the King James Version of the Christian Holy Bible:

Revelation 14:8 – And there followed another angel, saying, Babylon is fallen, is fallen, that great city, because she made all nations drink of the wine of the wrath of her fornication.

Revelation 17:5 – And upon her forehead was a name written, MYSTERY, BABYLON THE GREAT, THE MOTHER OF HARLETS AND ABOMINATIONS OF THE EARTH.

Revelation 18:2 – And he cried mightily with a strong voice, saying, Babylon the Great has fallen, is fallen, and has become the habitation of devils, and the hold of every unclean and hurtful bird.

Isaiah 21:9 – And, behold, here come a chariot of men, with a couple of horsemen. And he answered and said, Babylon is fallen, is fallen; and all the graven images of her gods he hath broken unto the ground.

Isaiah 48:14 – All ye assemble yourselves, and hear; which among them hath declared these things? The Lord hath loved them: He will do His pleasure on Babylon, and His arm shall be on the Chaldeans.

Jeremiah 51:8 – Babylon is suddenly fallen and destroyed; howl for her; take balm for her pain, if so be she may be healed.

Jeremiah 51:9 – We would have healed Babylon, but she is not healed; forsake her, and let us go everyone into his own country; for her judgment reacheth unto heaven, and is lifted up even to the skies.

Jeremiah 51:49 – As Babylon has caused the slain of Israel to fall, so at Babylon shall fall all the slain of all the earth.

Library definition: Thus, 'Babylon the Great' must be viewed as a symbolic city, one of which the literal city of Babylon was the prototype. Because the ancient city gives the mystic city its name, it is helpful to consider briefly the outstanding features of Babylon on the Euphrates, features that provide clues as to the identity of the symbolic city of the apostle John's vision provided in the Book of Revelation.

Dictionary definition of prototype: A first or earlier form from which other forms are developed or copied.

The name 'Babylon' is symbolic of the worlds nations in general, and considering their state of immorality and godlessness, that is the very world as it exists today (September 2024). Be assured that 'Babylon', or the Nations of the world, will fall. Just as was prophesied thousands of years ago. The degenerate state of being of almost all nations at present will bring about their destruction. Hence, Babylon (or the worlds nations) will fall by nuclear war or 'Nuclear Armageddon'!

Babylon was an ancient city that was overcome with sexual deviations and illicit sexual and false religion practices. Just as in the world's nations today, Babylon was a city or empire that had a dominating obsession of indulging in fornication and adultery. This situation, just as today, was enforced by military power and domination. The ruling elite used their power hold on the people in general by lies, hypocrisy and murder.

The minority elite of many nations today maintain their positions of power and wealth by trapping the unwary masses in psychological death traps of sexual fantasies and illicit pleasures triggered by acts of fornication and adultery and illicit drugs.

When individuals partake, they very soon develop an addiction. Almost immediately the suppliers demand servitude in the form of compromising one's ethics, standards, principles and moral values. Then when an individual commits acts of defiance against God, and bow to their oppressors acts of rebellion, they create a circumstance where they become in spiritual and temporal essence a 'Babylonish entity'. And 'Babylon' is going to fall!

'Fornication' is the deadly 'potion' that starts, maintains and finishes this secret demolition of human nature. This situation always leads to the Lord's punishment of 'the sword, the famine and the pestilence' that destroys nations.

The nations are extremely close to this happening right now. 'Babylon', and everyone in her, stand justly contemned!

CHAPTER 6

REACHING THE EDGE

On the Edge

Man Walking on a Boardwalk

We saints, as believers, are on the edge of the ultimate revelation. Or in other words, to grasp the fulness of our Creator's mysteries. I pray to our Creator, 'Jesus Christ', who gives us all our every heartbeat and every breathe we take, that He continue to expand our intellect to the point where we see and hear and understand all things pertaining to God and mankind.

I may not be a professor, engineer or philosopher, but just like most of you, I am very interested in meeting my Creator. From what I have learned over the years I write down a part, and I believe an important part, about the critical situation the world is in at present.

When an individual understands our Creator's works among mankind and creature on earth, one is on the road to being wise. Through much prayer and good works on our part, our Creator will elevate our intellect to the point where we understand all things pertaining to God's Creation. He will enlighten us to understand how He interacts with each individual's body and soul through our days of 'probation', hopefully in all cases to bring about that person's eventual 'eternal salvation'.

If a person is knowing and accepting of his or her inner workings, then are you endowed with knowledge of His presence inside your very body. And with appreciation and thankfulness, one should gladly thank their Lord and God. Through time and acceptability, you will gain wisdom and knowledge, even what is termed 'hidden wisdom and hidden knowledge'.

We are at the edge of being endowed with this gift, and in a short time I have faith that we will possess the mental intellect to understand all things pertaining to God and His Creation.

Capitalist System of Government

Wars are caused by unjust, unequitable, and at times, life losing, capitalist or socialist forms of government because they neglect the very God who created them in the first place. These different forms of government, without the blessing of their God, are doomed to failure. They all fail to provide for equality and therefore peaceful co-existence.

The capitalist and socialist ideologies are influential to the masses of all nations of injustice, immorality and ultimate friction between families and societies.

All forms of governments and peoples without God in them are doomed to failure from the start. They will end up with violence which always develops economically, socially, politically and militarily into a war situation.

The capitalist ideology, synonymous with 'Babylonish', when practiced by a nation or nations, always develops and evolves into war, violence and bloodshed.

At present in September 2024, the nations are perched at the doorstep of World War 3, and have evolved into this wholesale slaughter of millions of the innocent.

When World War 3 commences among the nations very soon, the socialist ideology nations will temporarily win, mainly because socialism begets brotherhood. But unfortunately for these temporary winners, only the chosen saints and believers will survive the ultimate war between God and the wicked of mankind. About a tenth of the present population of the world will survive as it states in Hebrew and Christian Scriptures.

Current Estate of Nuclear War Establishment

The spiritual and moral decadence and imminent collapse of modern generations of mankind has become a reality because of the rejection of truth and Christ. Far too many individuals indulge in blasphemous and sacrilegious, as well as rebellious behavior.

It is written in Holy Script: "It is not in mankind to direct their steps", and "It is God who gives us our very thoughts". When an individual disobeys Gods commandments, statutes and judgments, that person will find themselves doing so by a vengeful and just God. He will lead you to your destruction because of your rejection of His sovereignty, and because of your embrace of evil words and works.

The first step to salvation and blessings while in this path that leads to damnation is to break the chain of evil intentions and instead embrace your Creator whose Spirit dwells within your heart. It is called 'repentance', or stop committing evil deeds forever.

The next step, according to the Christian Gospel accounts, is 'baptism' in water signifying you have washed away your sins, and have publicly dedicated your life to Jesus Christ your personal Saviour.

The third step is 'endurance in your faith in Jesus Christ'. Over a short period of time in your life He will manifest Himself to you in the form of righteous words and deeds throughout the duration of the rest of your days forever.

Christ's presence in your heart and soul will guide your words and works throughout a violent, and unforgiving world with blessings and goodwill. You will have the contracted expectation of living forever in Paradise with your personal Saviour.

Jesus Christ (our God and Creator) will faithfully guide and direct your words and works to be holy and righteous throughout the rest of your life, both at present and forever thereafter in Heaven.

Present Realities in the Nations to Consider

- Western nations economies are failing.
- United States on the edge of being a failed state.
- The fall of the American dollar.
- Trillions of dollars spent on 'space race'.
- Trillions spent on the world's militaries.
- Immorality and injustice taking over nations.
- Nations ignoring chastity in favor of free love.
- A culture of violence and oppression.
- Severe lack of brotherly love in nations today.
- There exists a lack of compassion and empathy.
- Civilization is brutalized by mass culture of sex and violence.
- Most individuals at present are held captive to consumerism.
- The masses are exploited by the minority rich.
- 'Death Sleep' of the masses on earth at present leading to the 'impending doom'.
- Alcoholism and drug dependency cultures everywhere.
- Multiple direct warnings to all nations of 'World War 3' are ignored and laughed at!

CHAPTER 7

CALLING FOR HELP

Where to Find Help When

Student Friends Reading the Bible

Afraid: Psalm 4; Mark 4:35-41; Hebrews 13:5-8; 1 John 4:15-19.

Anxious: Psalm 46; Isaiah 43:1-3; Mathew 6:25-34; Philippians 4:6,7; 2 Timothy 4:16-18.

Backsliding: Psalm 6; Psalm 51; Matthew 26:33-35; Matthew 26:69-75; John 21:15-22.

Conscious of sin: Matthew 11:28-30; Luke 15; John 3:16.

Discouraged: Romans 8:28,29; 1 Corinthians 15:56-58; 1 Peter 4:12,13; 1 John 3:1-3.

Dismayed: Isaiah 41:10; Joshua 1:9.

Friends fail: Deuteronomy 33:27; Psalm 27; Matthew 10:24-31; 2 Timothy 4:16-18.

Hopeless: Romans 5:1-5.

Ill or in pain: Psalm 32; Psalm 91; Romans 5:3-8; 2 Corinthians 12:9,10.

Insecure: Isaiah 40:31, Psalm 84:11; John 1:9.

Leaving home: Psalm 27; Psalm 121; Matthew 10:16-20; Luke 15:11-32.

Lonely: Psalm 23; John 14; 1 Timothy 4:16-18.

Needing inward peace: Psalm 37; Isaiah 26:3; John 14; Romans 5:1-5.

In sorrow: Psalm 40; Romans 8:33-39; Hebrews 12:5-13.

In temptation: Psalm 1; Psalm 73; James 1:12; 2 Peter 2: 4-11.

Thankful: Psalm 84; Psalm 92; Psalm 100; Psalm 103.

In trouble: Psalm 16; Isaiah 40:1-8; John 14:1-4; Hebrew 7:25.

Under pressure: Isaiah 30:15; Isaiah 26:3.

Weary: Psalm 6; Psalm 27; Psalm 55; Matthew 11:28-30; John 14:1-4; Romans 8:31-39.

God loves you:
John 3:16 – For God so loved the world, that he gave his only begotten Son, that whosoever believeth in him should not perish, but have everlasting life.

All are sinners:
Romans 3:23 – For all have sinned and come short of the glory of God.

Romans 3:10 – As it is written, There is none righteous, no, not one.

God's remedy for sin:
Romans 6:23 – For the wages of sin is death, but the gift of God is eternal life through Jesus Christ our Lord.

John 1:12 – But as many as received Him, to them gave he the right to become the son of God, even to those that believe on His name.

1 Corinthians 15:3,4 – For I delivered unto you first of all that which I also received, how that Christ died for our sins according to the scriptures, and that he was buried, and that he rose again the third day according to the scriptures.

All may be saved now:
Revelation 3:20 - Behold, I stand at the door, and knock: if any man hear my voice, and open the door, I will come into him, and will sup with him, and he with me.

Life's Problems from the Teachings of Jesus Christ

Adversity – Matthew 10:16-39

Anger – Matthew 5:22-24

Bible reading – John 5:39; Matthew 24:35

Brotherly love – John 13:34;35

Compassion – Luke 10:30-37

Conceit – Luke 18:9-14

Crime – Matthew 15:11; 17-20

Death – Luke 16:19-31; John 11:25,26

Deceit – Matthew 23:27,28

Doubting – John 20:24-29

Enemies - Matthew 5:10, 43-48

Extravagance – Luke 12:16-31

Fault Finding – Matthew 7:1-5

Forgiveness – Matthew 18:21-35; Mark 11:25,26

Friendship – John 15:12,17

Greed – Luke 12:15-21; Matthew 6:20,21

Hatred – Matthew 5:43-48

Honesty – Luke 19:11-26

Honour to parents – Matthew 15:4; Mark 10:19

Intemperance – Luke 21:34-36

Marriage – Mark 10:2-12

Prayer – Luke 11:1-13

Revenge – Matthew 5:43-48

Riches – Mark 10:17-31; Luke 12:13-21

Righteousness – Matthew 5:20; John 3:13-21

Salvation – John 3:16; John 5:24

Sin – John 8:24; John 8:34-36

Sincerity – Matthew 7: 15-27

Swearing – Matthew 5:33-37

Truth – John 14:6

Suggested Readings

The creation story – Genesis 1

The fall of man – Genesis 3

Cain and Abel – Genesis 4:1-16

Noah's ark – Genesis 6:8

Lot – Genesis 19:1-28

Abraham offering Isaac – Genesis 22:1-18

Jacob's dream – Genesis 28:10-22

Moses – Exodus 1-4

Moses and Pharaoh – Exodus 5-12

Manna from heaven – Exodus 16:1-22

Sinai and the Ten Commandments – Exodus 19:16-25; 20:1-18

Joshua – Joshua 1

Rahab and the spies – Joshua 2

Crossing the Jordan – Joshua 3

The conquest of Jericho – Joshua 6

Gideon – Judges 6,7

Samson – Judges 13:5-25; 14:1-16

Ruth's choice – Ruth 1-4

The call of Samuel – 1 Samuel 3

David and Goliath – 1 Samuel 17

Mephibosheth – 2 Samuel 9

Solomon and the Queen of Sheba – 1 Kings 10

Ellijah – 1 Kings 17,18

Elisha – 2 Kings 4,5

Esther the Queen – Esther 1-9

Daniel's friends in the furnace – Daniel 3

Belshazzar's feast – Daniel 5

Daniel in the lion's den – Daniel 6

Jonah – Jonah 1-4

Prophesies of suffering and death of Jesus Christ – Psalm 22; Isaiah 53

The birth of Jesus Christ – Matthew 1:18-25; 2:1-12

The temptation of Jesus Christ – Luke 4:1-13

Sermon on the mount – Matthew 5-7

Some miracles performed – Matthew 8,9; Mark 6:30-56; Mark 7:24-30; John 9

Some parables told – Matthew 13; Matthew 21:28-46; 22:1-14; Matthew 24; Mark 4:1-34; Luke 12:16-59; 13:1-17; 18:1-14; 19:12-27

The ministry of Jesus Christ – Luke 4:18,19

Jesus speaks of the 'bread of life' – John 6:22-59

Jesus speaks of the 'good shepherd' – John 10:1-18

Jesus Christ's promise to return again, address on the 'mount of olives' – Matthew 24,25

The Last Supper – Luke 22:1-39

The trial of Jesus Christ – Matthew 26:57-75; 27:1-26

Jesus Christ is crucified – Luke 23:26-56

The Lord Jesus lives again – Luke 24:1-48

Ministry of the risen Jesus Christ – Matthew 28:9-20

Jesus ascends to heaven – Acts 1:1-11

Peter's sermons – Acts 2:14-41; Acts 3:11-26

The first martyr, Stephen's address and stoning – Acts 6:8-15; 7:1-60

The conversion of Paul – Acts 9:1-22

Paul's first sermon – Acts 13:16-41

Paul in prison – Acts 16:23-40

Paul's sermon in Athens – Acts 17:22-34

Paul's defense before king Agrippa – Acts 26:1-29

Paul in a storm and shipwreck – Acts 27

Becoming a Christian – Romans 10:9-13

Christian life and service – Romans 12,13

The testing of faith – James 1,2

Christian love and faith – 1 John 4:7-21; 5:1-15

The resurrection of Christ and Christians – 1 Corinthians 15:1-57

Jesus Christ comes on earth again – 2 Peter 3:1-18; Revelation 19:11-19

The Final Judgment and the end of Satan – Revelation 19:20,21; 20:1-15

Glimpses of Heaven and the Glory of God – Revelation 21:1-27; 22:1-5

The Seven Deadly Sins

Pride
Gluttony
Envy
Greed
Laziness
Lust
Wrath

Seven Virtues

Diligence
Humility
Generosity (charity)
Meekness
Chastity
Liberality (temperance)
Forgiveness (kindness)

The Seven Social Sins

"Wealth without work" – Acquisition or retention of unjust wealth.

"Pleasure without conscience" – Society without love.

"Knowledge without character" – Perpetuation of ignorance.

"Commerce without morality" – Industry and business without morality.

"Science without Humanity" – Civilization lost.

"Religion without Sacrifice" – Abuse of Creation.

"Politics without Principle" – Politics of fear, hate or exclusion.

Christian Virtues and Character

Cheerfulness – Philippians 4:4; Colossians 3:16,17

Cleanliness – 2 Corinthians 7:1

Courage – Philippians 1:27,28

Diligence – Romans 12:10-13

Discretion – Ephesians 5:15-17

Endurance – 2 Timothy 2:3

Faith – Mark 11:22-24

Faithfulness – 1 Corinthians 4:2

Forgiveness – Ephesians 4:31,32

Friendliness – Romans 12:15,18

Gratitude – Philippians 4:6

Honesty – Romans 12:17

Honour – 1 Peter 2:17

Humility – Philippians 2:3-11

Liberality – 2 Corinthians 9:6-15

Love – 1 John 4:7,8

Meekness – Matthew 5:5

Mercy – Matthew 5:7

Obedience – Romans 13:1-7

Patience – Hebrews 10:36,37

Peacefulness – Romans 12:18

Prudence – James 1:19

Pure thinking – Philippians 4:8

Purity – 2 Timothy 2:22

Steadfastness – Ephesians 6:10-20

Sympathy – 1 Peter 3:8,9

Temperance – 1 Corinthians 9:25-27

Truthfulness – Ephesians 4:14-16, 25,29

END

POSTSCRIPT

Why I have Always Believed in God

I realized as a young man that the universe is infinite, it has no outer edges. That there exists no central point anywhere in the universe, from which one could measure to the outer edge. Before the physical and material universe was created, or came into existence, there did exist only one thing, and that is infinitely dark and empty, supernatural space. No beginning or ending of time and space. Only complete infinite nothingness, and that is a 'supernatural' state of being and existence. And that 'supernatural' was a 'Being', and possessed self awareness of His own existence. A supernatural 'Being' or God or Creator (as mankind calls Him). In ancient Hebrew scriptures that 'Creator', or infinitely supernatural 'Being' was called 'Jehovah'. That Creator became flesh when He, by miraculous conception, was born of the virgin Mary about 2,000 years ago. He took upon Himself the personal name of "Jesus Christ". He became an infinitely intimate extension of His supernatural self 'Jehovah'. And dwelt for all eternity, past, present and future, forever in the heavens. We humans dwell in the flesh and only exist at Jesus Christ's power and will. Christ, our infinite Creator, lends us humans His 'supernatural light and life'. And we exist in the flesh and we become self oriented to exercise 'free will' to choose to acknowledge and accept our 'Creator', or reject Him outrightly. Jesus Christ, our infinite, omnipotent and omnipresent Creator, maintains our every thought and deed from the time we are conceived in our mother's womb. Therefore Jesus Christ, our Creator and infinite God, claimed and states about Himself that He is the 'Light and the Life' of all the members of mankind since Adam and Eve were first created. And so it is, a fact and true reality, from the beginning and to the ending, of the creation cosmic epoch!

APPENDIX

Over the millennium many nations have invented and fabricated numerous gods and goddesses to comfortably fit into their social, cultural, political and religious norms.

In theological and cosmological rational reasoning, I offer the following shortened explanation of the origins of the universe and of the universe's Creator and God, our Lord Jesus Christ.

In the beginning, the very beginning before anything existed, a reality of something did exist of 'oneness of infinite nothingness'. No length, no width, no height or depth, no volume but the volume of infinite nothingness. So 'one infinite nothingness' was a reality of existence.

So 'one' infinite nothingness of space did in reality exist. And the 'one', He was a projection of infinity of the first stages of intellectual being, although in the very, very first phase of the cosmic epoch called the creation.

This very first phase was in 'dimness', but in the evolutionary discipline of spiritual growth, God said "Let there be Light!", as it states in the Christian Holy Bible.

This is the only explanation I can imagine (or that the good Lord has given me) of where God or Christ came from. Because it would have been utterly impossible for anything to come into existence in infinite and empty nothingness, except by intelligent design.

Milton Keynes UK
Ingram Content Group UK Ltd.
UKHW020642171124
2889UKWH00016B/38

9 798385 036493